fata morgana

Joel Chace

Unlikely Books
www.UnlikelyStories.org
New Orleans, Louisiana

fata morgana

For Candy, Larissa, Logan, Brechyn, Tristan , and Oana.

Contents

seeds

Reading Jack Spicer

Skinny paper slips
months ago stuffed, forgotten,
now loosen from the book's
center, flutter across
a blue comforter.
In green: to get good, this
glow, restaurant, weapon,
the latch, nowhere. In red:
I'm X, means that. In
yellow: shore, loop,
listen like hell.
Scattered over blue.

I'm X means that I
listen like hell: ___________________________________ *Vellutello proposed new figures
                                                      for the height of Lucifer,
                                                      triangulated from the circumference
                                                      of the earth, the height of the giants
                                                      and the distance of Hell's lowest circles.*

                    on
the yellow shore where
green birds step and breezes
bring tears; in any
restaurant where whisperings
are a red wind; in traffic
loops, radio static ___________________________ *The complex spectrum with rising and
                                                 falling tones is very similar
                                                 to Earth's auroral emissions.*

a blue circulation.
I listen like
hell to get good again.

This glow ____*An electron moving in a medium*
does radiate light even if it is
moving uniformly provided
that its velocity is greater than the
velocity of light in the medium.

           from the red
planet. A radio
plays in a furnished, latched
room. Listen. If you don't
like hell, ____*I think that you'll never enter*
Bohemia...but for poetry — to
see the windows and maybe blast a few
yourself through the rocks of hell. I'll be
there waiting for you, my arms open.

           move. Somewhere. Nowhere.
Just take a weapon along.

When any center ____*A box-and-whisker*
plot provides a visual
way of understanding both
the range and the middle.

        scatters,
colors switch: red with
yellow; blue with green. Latches
begin to click; newspaper
ink rewinds; comforters
flutter — X ____*When while becomes*
infinite —
while(y<10)
x=x+1:
end
No
end.

      — to a
new job; forgotten
others head to the shore
by all necessary means.

That restaurant gives
as good as it takes. Across
the highway a farmer
walks among his cows. He's
proud they're skinny, not stuffed; in
truth, he sees their gauntness ________________________*...white snow and leafless trees, and a*
winding track; but close to the sledge
were three dark wasted animals...

as a weapon. Once
he latches his barn doors,
the beasts inside start
a green glow. ________________________*For the delicate task of applying*
the paint to the tiny dials, the women were
instructed to point the brushes with
their lips. They became known as Radium Girls.

       Basking in it,
yonder, the diners smile.

Loop-d-loop; lie-d-lie. Months
later, still no knowledge, ________________________...*language is...a knowing, an event...*
                                                      as words are important to hold on to
                                                      whatever it is that composes us.

nor nowhere, nor all the
bluebooks in the world. Getting
good means finding that island,
squatting near the green
sea, deciphering
octopus ____...*three hearts*
                                                      and blue blood...

      ink.
Loop-d-loop; lie-d-lie.
A comfort: slip of the tongue.

From Mars

"Reading Jack Spicer" is a consequence of my reading Jack Spicer, specifically his seminal collection *My Vocabulary Did This to Me*, a book that I've read, returned to, and reread over decades. My most recent encounter began months ago, in the long-long-time-ago, pre-covid days. When I opened the text, ten to twelve thin, short strips of paper fluttered down into my lap. Right away, I recognized them as remnants from a visual poetry project completed years earlier. Why they'd ended up in that book, I've no recollection. However, as I looked over the single words and phrases originally printed in tiny fonts of different colors -- the words and colors that I reference in the first section of my poem -- it seemed strangely yet wonderfully appropriate that those messages had been delivered to me as if from Jack's Martians. I couldn't possibly refuse them.

The italicized, right hand commentary riffing off the key seed words is a method I'd just started to employ in previous writings. It's a procedure that fell into my head, also serendipitously.

Seeds

You'll probably want to see
this, the archive of every
unsaid sentence. In night's
icy font: seed-hoe
with tattered diploma nailed
to its handle; daily
bread; kitchen table and
restless hands; already
drying, dying tongues;
the tiniest
circles ever. That could
be one. This might be
another — *Here comes*
a copper to bop off
your head. Or, How can
a preview hurt?

So someone tells the
faster-than-the-speed-of-light
joke, while restless regulars
study their cards, never
guessing what's buried right
beneath. Talk about
a preview. ____*With practice, it should be possible
to detect patterns or peaks which might
even suggest the nature and potential
date, time and place of a disaster.*

       The upshot
being that it arrived before
getting there. Ass's jawbone,
ancient giant curled into
a seed, ________________________________*They belonged to the Judean Date Palm species,
which had been a staple crop for thousands of years
but became extinct by 500AD after
the Romans wiped them out in an
attempt to cripple the Jewish economy.*

      circle of torn-out
hair, assbone of a
fool, half a heart.

Take physics, pomp. And having
in earliest sections
referenced the over-arching
title does not entail
continuance or even
previews. ________________________________*It would be wrong for me to say that I was not*
frightened by a prediction of this nature.
I intend keeping a diary from now on and to
record my reactions to this on a daily
basis. I suppose anybody who plays about
with precognition in this way to some extent
sticks his neck out and must accept what he gets.

       Dust, glows,
rushings, other
wonders. Widening
sanctuaries ______________________________________*No longer could they take*
refuge behind the temple walls.

      become
possible. One could even
speak about pieces of air.

A voice grows louder
in the street. A window in
the third story shoots up. As
those tongues ________________________________*The new brain scans contrasted*
sharply with images taken of
other spiritually-inspired
mental states like meditation.

        in the street
grow louder, a window
shoots up three stories
above. When they tire
of learning, they say so. Which,
supposedly, is
good. Which? good? Demarcating
alleluias from
rapture, the sundial, _________________________*It was found on the floor of a*
workman's hut in the Valley of the Kings.

        in her
garden, the sundial
demarcates alleluias
from raptures.
So. So. Tired.

More often lately, the bus
overshoots their stop. Line
of tiny circles along
the road's shoulder. The familiar
hoe leaning against its tree,
sundial, ____*In time, Egyptians made them*
portable, smaller
versions of the obelisks.

       ground ivy. Someone has
bequeathed them that house, which never
comes closer for all their trudging.
In the story, a heartbreaking ______________________*The normal organ appears as if it has*
literally been broken and the left
ventricle stretches out to form
a narrow neck-shaped section.

ceremony at the end.

Fitting in easier next time,
right? Jagged chunks of classroom
buildings, archives, _______________________________ *Native diggers sold*
piecemeal what they found there.

             explode over
the campus lawns, but no one
really to blame.   Can't be too much
to ask: gliding a half-inch
above hallowed pathways; ink
already drying on the
diploma. Sanctuary _______________________________ *That scene with Jaweh walking*
in the cool of the garden.

             soon
to shrink in the rearview
mirror for the final time.

In the instructors' parlor,
students, restless. One way to
dig up trouble but avoid
police. They do keep on
trying though they think of it as
a living room and of themselves
as a half-circle of tiny
easels. Like windows shooting
up, words rise — rupture,
rapture? air barrage,
arbitrage? ____*?E(R) I? = E(R)z ?+ (E(I) ? E(R)z?) × ?n*
       Those teachers seem
intimate yet rather
pruney as though submerged too
long in the font. ______________________________________*Nobody knows why it had been*
covered and put in this place and
never written about
in any historical book.

       One draws
the students while the other
draws out of them
such as may be cleaned.

To practice arbitrage ________________________*So, there is no doubt that this, in theory,*
is something that can be a great benefit
to the investors as well as the traders.

          by
the river bank. Later he stood
and rose up on a
dictionary that covered
a stunned bat. So use that word
in a sentence. Seizing the day,
or rather the carp, ________________________*If the carp successfully makes the jump*
over the mythical Gate, it
transforms into a powerful dragon.

        only
long enough to unhook and
release it. Now that word
has been used in this sentence.

Burst pod: dark seeds ________________________________ *They grew but did not at all look*
like the picture she sent. We were
completely devastated.

              flecking
a cloudy white that clings to tufts
of fur on the forest floor. So.
Another mystery
born. Grows. Summon the
unusual testifiers.
All quite enough to make one
wail. Enough to shake
one's heart. Enough to split a
heart in two, ________________________________ *Takotsubo Cardiomyopathy is*
the medical term.

        then
break each half.

They did whatever it took
to get out of weeding. Angling for carp,   _____*It used to be said that only seventy*
could make the climb in any year. When the first
succeeded, then the rains would begin to fall.

       much cooler business.
Later, under duress, they
testified that their sloth had been
weaponized. Strange, rising word.

Archivist ____*Most of the time we cannot tell whether
we are dealing with an archival aggregate or a
collection of trash, the equivalent
of a modern waste-paper basket*

       of licenses, she
frequently observed that
a cleaver could cleave a carp ____________________*I shall transcend the estate of ordinary
fish and achieve a place among the order of
sacred dragons. I shall rid myself forever
of the terrible suffering to which
my race is heir, expunge every trace
of our shame and humiliation.*

but then could not cleave it. Fatty
Arbuckle ____*At some point, Arbuckle and Rappe ended
up together in a bedroom, from where,
minutes later, her screams were heard.*

       might very well
have kept his own scrapbook. That was
another fish flopping and
drying in the dirt. Dead
people, and broken things.

When he offers to eat a
crocodile, it's like, O.K.,
we get it; he really does
love her. What Gertrude did know,
and when she did know it. So
many tongues ______________________________*Based on a recent study of nearly*
1,000 evangelicals,
researchers have identified at least
two forms of the practice, one ecstatic and
frenzied, the other subdued and nearly silent.

       lolling in
the promise-crammed air. And what, at
the end, they both did
finally know. And even
Arbuckle, ____*Acquittal is not enough*
for Roscoe Arbuckle.

    for that
matter. Dead and broken, all.

Redeeming avocations:
digging up jawbones, grabbing
tapestries of air. Breath in a
wide sanctuary, ____*Silence isn't the*
absence of something but
the presence of everything.

        hair rings,
fonts, ____*They were astonished*
to find the one
so long sought after hidden
inside another.

    crocodile necklaces,
sundial bracelets. Judges
sustain secrets and say, Quashed.
Testimony becomes them.

Freshly-weeded, seeded
lawns, one beyond the other
until they make tiny
circles. Freshly-cleaved carp
ready in the kingdom's
freezers. All regulars
released, permitted raptures
and alleluias, then
rounded back up once the
sundial's first shadow falls. Less
bequest than testament.
Less tongue itself than words.

fata morgana

fata morgana

Corridor in — in a
lake. Hallway _________________________________*The relationship between philosophy and*
architecture is inter-
rogative and propositional. It
is about asking questions concerning the
meaning of human ha-
bitation.

at lake-bottom. Of
water: ceiling, walls,
floor where he moves ___________________________________*...that the main task of arch-*
itecture is the interpretation
of a way of life...

forward, with clip-
board, pen. On each side,
watery doors ___________________________________*They do not last long, but change as*
the vapors in which they ap-
pear, from one place to another.

open, hands thrust
documents towards him.
He signs, signs,
advances, signs. That
corridor. That life.

There's a way up,
out, one path____*Its implicit admission that all*
this may be a put-on, may not
be worth your while. The poi-
gnancy of this situation
heightens our response.

up from the cor-
ridor, but
he's so tired.

In a raised well. A
clear, invisible ____ *And although these colors have left*
no visible traces of themselves,
they nevertheless burn in-
sidiously in the non-
color that has replaced them.

well brought up into
light, into a space. As if
he speaks from within a
column of glass air. As ____________________ *The whole mountain was in a trembling*
motion; one part collapsed and left
behind a great valley; a new
peak arose, higher than before;
and next to this se-
veral others, cone-shaped,
but immediately as-
summed the form of immense rectangular
towers, which likewise tumbled in
a moment and opened huge valleys.

if he is a Banquo come
back to tell them he
didn't deserve twenty
mortal murders on his
head, that he can just
barely be in their
world anymore, that those
he returns to instruct or ____________________ *In one and the same act, philosophy*
and architecture enclose man in
their shell and structure, and dis-
close open vistas, new ho-
rizons, spiritual

*possibilities of expansion
and self-realization.*

murder will not stay murdered
or instructed, unlike
a Banquo who returns but
cannot be unmur-
dered or stay for long in
the well in the light, ___________________________*In this same sea, yet another won-
der: when the storm ceases and the air
becomes still, at dawn,
changing images of an-
imals and men in the air.*

that well, raised up.

When it rises, ____ *Thus, the final stand-*
ard of architectural val-
ue for some is the ethical.

he spends weeks huf-
fing from one gleaming hallway
to the next, never
certain, arriving minutes
after others had given ________________________________*Some are quite motion-*
less, some run through the air, some
fight among themselves, and last e-
ven until the Sun gains strength,
in whose heat all disappear.

up and left: too many cor-
ners; too many stairs. ________________________________*We should evaluate build-*
ings according to how well
they make possible de-
sired forms of life.

Odd room to enter: re-
dolent of a-
bandonment even ____*Some plea-*
sure is really
something else: to name
it would be to see it va-
nish.

when occupied. Each day
a palimpsest of air
hangs, with the last
layer fluttering be- ______________________________________*They soon climbed to 2 degrees*
height, but then began
to take on man-
ifold forms, and this disp-
lay convinced me that they
were something quite
different from clouds.

hind once the final
visitor departs. Then
he wanders to a bank of
windows. Early-winter,
late-afternoon gray
reflects steeples and lights down
in the village back into
the space at his back, to which
he turns, thinking, "Is design
luck's residue? Is it time
for a new philosophy
of rooms that deserve ___________________________*Philosophy and architecture have*
the coming task of hea-
ling the split of knowledge and

sorrow? Is there nothing in
the dark that's not
there in the light?"

Whole side of the old
building, whole old side, falls ________________________ *There is a power to fix for*
eternity the disappearance
of that which pre-
sents itself, or the
power to prod-
uce presence itself
as Idea.

outward. He
stands directly in
the collapse-path. What smashes
over him — a large window ________________________ *Standing at the casement,*
finally saw it, a mountain ri-
sing from the sea about 60
Italian miles away, like
a dark-blue cloud.
I became ve-
ry uneasy.

pane, his still upright
body exactly at its
center. All the shards that ________________________ *They aren't all-*
usions or comments,
however ob-
lique; they are themselves
what is ha-
ppening.

scatter do him no harm: the
weather frigid; his heavy
cap and coat prevent
even the tiniest scratch.

42

the plague year

Return of Plague Year Narrative

The great rolling came
from afar but was
soon upon us while some

were still shaping sentences.   *Nudge it a little*
more that way.
                    What's the price
on that?
        There'll be a guy
over tomorrow to do
an inspection.
                    What exactly
are you trying to say?

Those were ones.
An article on

a woman who
had just started labor
but stopped herself and refused

to participate until
someone who wasn't even
there agreed to leave

the room. That caused a
stir. A slew of old songs
began re-echoing, many

of them unfortunate.
People published
lists. ____*Pin, recalibration, plain
*white foundation, reagent,
bluing, string.*

    *Acknowledgement,
dirt, rectangle, flour,
tubing, bell, greening,
stalk.*

    *Candle, mask, count,
yellowing, tongue.*

Those were ones.

Sky-high. Concussive. Wave.
Houses turned into

triangles. Stories about
people inside. ____*A body in fire. Her
body in a fire.*

*Embodiment
of fire. Fire burns*

*her voice, but he
doesn't understand.*

*Misunderstanding, a
fire consuming like*

no other. Her eyes in
fire. Her words silent

in fire. Her body
hardens in fire. Her

eyes harden in fire. The
flames of her eyes try

to be words, a voice
he doesn't comprehend.

Gown for night. Gown of
night. Her final

gown. Her skin in fire strains
up from inside

the fabric. Fire gown. He fingers
its cotton, then walks

upstairs, leaving
her with the tiny

fire-bellied toad
of poisonous properties.

That was
one. All
undone.
Hardly
begun.

Hunting

Same order: advance the
winnowing. _____________________________*During the present*
                                          order, intercession
                                          for the weak is possible.

          All up and down
ranks, chosen people step
back into their own
shadows. What's required includes
collecting each severed ______________________*…our blood-guiltiness toward*
                                          animals tries
                                          to find release…

animal leg left next to
its trap. Searchers _______________________*Suddenly, as though a cloud*
                                          came over the sun, the air
                                          was cold and the noise died
                                          down to a twittering of
                                          birds. Men and women looked
                                          about, everyone silent.

          must proceed
at a general's double-arm's
length. Light now slants through
the woods.
          So…They return
to garrison.
          So…With
minds a-stutter, hearts in

tatters. ____...*a confused crowd of others*
in curious or ragged
clothes, and all had their eyes
fixed with the same look…

      They'll sleep,
wake.
      Tomorrow,
same order.

Fishing

Early-April. This one
screams.   *...they occupy a part of the*
soundscape that had
previously been assumed...
irrelevant to
human communication.

            Smacks lake-water with his
right hand. Drags his already
drowned brother with his left. This
one, screaming, wants to drive
a nail through icy water.
To nail it quickly to
shore. To bring them
instantly there, him
and his already dead
carpenter   *...stretcheth out his rule...*
marketh it out with a
line...fitteth it with
planes...marketh it out
with the compass, and maketh it
after the figure of a man,
according to the beauty
of a man; that it may remain
in the house.

            brother. Whom he
pulls. Away from the

already sunken boat. ______________________________*The catch had rapidly changed*
in shape and size from pretty
one-pound trout, to great-eyed,
loose-mouthed, cod-like monsters piled
high in a horrible heap.

      Toward

that nightmare, far.
Fixed ____*...being in a void that is*
rumbling deeply like
an airplane engine attached,
with all its awful
weight, to the head...

    shore.

Mourning Dove

Song of dust, of
desiccation, that mutes all
others, its volume more
of suasion ________________________________*After many attempts of*
asking his sister to share
the fish with him, he transforms
into a bird and flies
away, singing while crying,
creating a melody
of abandonment.

            than of sound.
Fallen melody,
falling.
      Attends to
loss.
      Annunciates ________________________________*…in musical tones, being,*
existence, is
indistinguishable from,
is, pointing-beyond-itself,
meaning, saying.

      it.

Home

In the loved place. ____ *…during which one*
realizes that people
with money are the favored
in life's competitions.

Keeping wanting. Sibling ________________________________ *…a goad that practices*
on you and you
can't get rid of…

                              in
the loved place. Keeping to
leave. Sibling ________________________________ *…what a strange creature…*

                    says,
"Stay in darkness. ________________________________ *…has always got there*
first, and is waiting.

Eat." Sibling's invitation.
In place. ________________________________ *…elementary*
realities reveal that
they are not confined…that they
partake less than the nature
of being than that of
language and can compel
whatever is beside them
to speak…of an
unforeseeable future.

"Stay. Consume. Eat
darkness. ____ *This is the story…in*
a cave….head
encased in concrete.

All of it."

Reading

Near the end of that
story, ________________________________...*if the words are not right, what is said is*
not what is meant. If what is said is not
meant, work cannot flourish. If work
does not flourish, then customs and arts
degenerate. If customs
and arts degenerate, then justice
is not just. If justice is not just, the
people do not know what to do. Hence,
the importance that words be right.

       the fat boy with a
silver stallion ________________________________*And the sun is gonna*
burn into a cinder
before we ever pass
this way again.

on his red sweatshirt
accompanies them — injured,
nameless mother; nameless
infant; nasty little
June Star — ________________________________*"I don't want to hold*
hands with him…He
reminds me of a pig."

       into the woods. Moments
after — scream, gunshot. Shot.
Shot.
       Ought it pay
a reader to reflect
upon the order in which

those three murders occur? _______________________________ *"Shut up, Bobby Lee," The Misfit said. "It's no real pleasure in life."*

Clothing

They lied, those
memories of stuffing
garments ____...discards every trace
                                                    of noble attire and
                                                    elegance to become
                                                    an unworthy member...

          into bags,
hauling them away.
                    Stepping
into this closet — _______________________________...opening up a
                                                    door for the word...

               maybe
for a final visit — _______________________________The doom is nearer
                                                    now: it is at
                                                    the door; it has
                                                    lifted the latch.

               here
they are, back on hangers, jammed
tighter than ever, dense
as the tar baby, _________________________________...just sat...looking as cute
                                                    as a button and
                                                    saying nothing at all.

          as
the briar patch. _________________________________Drown me! Roast me!
                                                    Hang me! Do
                                                    whatever you please...

                    Impossible
to penetrate or
even to turn around.

Motions

About to step ____ *...fidgeting as if the ground*
beneath had suddenly
become unbearably hot...

         forward
and down. Peripheral ______________________________________ *...untethered, its*
primary concern...
advancement...

flash. Swirl of
white and red.
Vision-tapestry. ____ *...and, above, is the*
Pentecostal wind...presence
of the Holy Spirit...

       White.
Red. The dead, reckoning _________________________________ *What do they have*
to do, turn inside
out to make you see?

          they're
well out of it. A
snowflake capping each
holly ____ *...ruler of the white*
realm, king of the
darker half of the year.

    berry, each prick
of blood.
      Now — forward,
down — the step.

Transport

A trestle that trembled…____*When the No. 38*
eased over…the
sensation was more akin
to ballooning
than to railroading.

and held its ties, rails, trains _______________________________*10,000 sleds dispatched*
one day from a toy works.

       that

trembled it, ____*The shaking could be felt at*
the north end of the high
girders when a train entered
the south end, around
half a mile away.

    while it held
together this
landscape. Beneath the space
that held its trestle, a dark,
rushing stream.

Money

Bones bright
under sun, brighter
beneath moon. ____*In lunar light,*
on a chariot made of
bones of the dead, he
drove at furious speed.

                    Silver-fingered
Tell-Tale taps ____*...very, very dreadfully*
nervous…but why…
say that I am mad?

          softly,
insistently, at the
door. So much out here. Something
called a coin gleaming on
the sidewalk. Another, here. Five
more. Come on. Out, and bring your
own gamble-bones. _______________________________*…fashioned from the ankles*
of sheep, marked on four sides, used
as magical devices
that could predict the
future…Casting lots, a way
of saying this decision
is beyond human
intelligence. Let's
ask a god.

               Capital
idea.

Amusement

Plan's afoot to cross
the river, ____*Almost without*
realizing it, I went
from my boat to this other
mysterious boat. And
suddenly I understood…
the meaning of existence.

          to storm those park
gates that the dead have guarded
for months. Demands of the
living, most natural: fried
dough; cover bands; to stream — once
more — aboard
a mammoth,
rocking pirate ship. ____________________________*But in a minute she 'gan stir,*
With a short uneasy motion—
Backwards and forwards half her length
With a short uneasy motion.

Then like a pawing horse let go,
She made a sudden bound:
It flung the blood into my head,
And I fell down in a swound.

       Next day,

they'll wake, happier, dumber, _______________________ *Then Daniel took pitch, fat,*
and hair, and boiled them
together and made cakes, which
he fed to the dragon. The
dragon ate them and burst
open. And Daniel said, "See
what you have been worshipping!"

awaiting their shift before
re-padlocked gates. Demands of
the dead: a spoon and rattle
to shake; scarecrow,
thorn bush, corpse.

Autopsy

Blubberous waist of shame
cloven, so that those silly
legs teeter on his golden
swimming raft, and tip, dragging
their appendages into
the lake. ____*...suddenly looked at each
other with mutual
understanding…realizing
that they were eating the person
who had been drowned and had been pulled
out of the water by a fork.*

        Monstrous upper
body, a squadron of
kindly angels ____*...and do not hide
yourself when he
has become a corpse…*

     somehow
snatches, mid-air, ____*Be certain that
none of his words are
covered by the waters.*

      and freights
to shore. There, arms macheted,
also head, which — oddly
light — ____*...in the continual
service of cleansing the
language of all fixations
upon dead, stinking dead,
usages of the past.*

          rolls down into oozy
mud. Torso, Y'd open;
ribcage, pried and snapped
apart. At last, cut
free, the still cooling,
meant-to-be sacred
muscle. Now, anatomizing,

pondering ____*TO POOR TOM*
                                                  Thou robed man of justice, take thy place;

                                                  TO THE FOOL
                                                  And thou, his yoke-fellow of equity,
                                                  Bench by his side:

                                                  TO KENT

                                                          you are o' the commission,

                                                  sit you too.

          can begin: what
breeds, what makes, this hard heart?

Retirement

O, for those days that began
with dust motes treading air, flashing
in light that slanted through the
room, onto faces of
students. ______________________________________

...so a lot of people were
burned or hanged or their heads
were cut off because of this
yoiking tradition, and still
today…in the most Lappish
areas, there are laws
forbidding teachers to instruct
their charges how to yoik.

   Those days when some
slumped in seats, or conversed
easily, not quietly. Days
when it seemed their number had
tripled over night. ______________________________________

...and the Demon, crying out,
"Here's your year — here are all
the horrors that have happened
to you and that are still going to
happen," then dragged out a
succession of limp, black,
squirming things and threw them
on the floor before me...

    Days when
none attended to the one
paid, actually, to bring
them all along. When that

one at last divined
that, actually, the only
recourse was killing. ____ *There is a great negative*
work of destruction to be
done. Cleaning. Sweeping. The
cleanliness of
the individual
asserts itself after the state
of madness…

                    When murder,

slashing, ____ *…going systematically*
to work smashing every
connotation that words
ever had, in order to
get them back clean.

       became the order
of business. When, each
evening, knowledge dawned: all
must be annihilated,
the exact same destroyed ________________________________ *Subversion is the very*
movement of writing:
that of death.

                once
more, along with daily extras.

Abeyance

Their unerring sense for
what comes next: Elgar
with his hunter; ____*The beginning is laden*
with anticipation.

           Vaughn
Williams with his lark. ______________________________________E, G, A, B, D
                                                             (1, 3, 4, 5, 7)

           For what
must come next.

But what, when
nothing comes next?

Abeyance: no ascent; ____ *The basis of his work is the*
line: a melody with
a visionary
quality and a broad
humanity.

                     whole
sweep of all the lawns, with their
mucky goldfish ponds. Pressing,

hard, forearms against high
windows. So much
out there. But no descent. _______________________________*…a tendency toward downward*
leaps, often of a seventh,
giving its line a sharply
serrated profile…

Black surface of the fallen _______________________________________*...free sweep*
                                                          of the line, scorning
                                                          to rest on accents...

river: town-lights ripple, flash,
on and along.
            Suspended,

crossing the water, gray-black
pavement; same neon,
illuminated windows,

tv screens.
            And, rising, ___________________________________*Orchestra*
                                                          and violin
                                                          soloist express
                                                          the metaphysical
                                                          states of being and
                                                          becoming, respectively.

thin, thin arc of
dark casting

its brightest points
on pavement, on river.
                    No
one out there, to see.

Street once more
empty except for two
guys running behind the dark
maw of a garbage truck. One
picks up a can, hustles

over, hands it to
the other who hurls its
contents into the blackness,
screams, "Thank you!" then passes it
back to the first, who

returns the "Thank you!" So on,
until the curb-man gets
to a load he can't lift. "This
is a fucking
bear!" So his buddy steps

up. And once it's dispatched,
they face each
other. "Thank you!"
Company policy? Only
a lark? ____*...chirrup, whistle, slur and shake.*

Ascent? ____*...resolving the disjunction*
                                                 of the material and
                                                 the spiritual...

Descent? ___________________________________*It undulates, but it is
the sound of all things coming
together as one.*

        But
somehow language is
here. Even
in the street.
Especially.

Acknowledgments

All poems in this collection have previously appeared in the following publications: *Eratio, Ex-Ex-Lit, Golden Handcuffs Review, Litter, Otoliths*, and *Word For/Word*. Sincere thanks to the editors for their kind permission to reprint.

About the Author

Joel Chace has published work in print and electronic magazines such as *Eratio, Otoliths, Word For/Word,* and *Golden Handcuffs Review.* Most recent collections include *Scorpions,* from Unlikely Books, *Humors,* from Paloma Press, and *Threnodies,* from Moria Books.

Recent Books by Joel Chace

Threnodies (Moria Books, 2019)

Humors (Paloma Press, 2018)

Scorpions (Unlikely Books, 2016)

War, and After (BlazeVOX [books], 2016)

matter no matter (Paper Kite Press, 2008)

Cleaning the Mirror: Selected and New Poems (BlazeVOX [books], 2007)

Uncertain Relations (Birch Brook Press, 2000)

Recent Titles from Unlikely Books

Typescenes by Rodney A. Brown

Political AF: A Rage Collection by Tara Campbell

The Deepest Part of Dark by Anne Elezabeth Pluto

Swimming Home by Kayla Rodney

Manything by dan raphael

Citizen Relent by Jeff Weddle

The Mercy of Traffic by Wendy Taylor Carlisle

Cantos Poesia by David E. Matthews

Left Hand Dharma: New and Selected Poems by Belinda Subraman

Apocalyptics by C. Derick Varn

Pachuco Skull with Sombrero: Los Angeles, 1970 by Lawrence Welsh

Monolith by Anne McMillen (Second Edition)

When Red Blood Cells Leak by Anne McMillen (Second Edition)

My Hands Were Clean by Tom Bradley (Second Edition)

anonymous gun. by Kurtice Kucheman (Second Edition)

Soy solo palabras but wish to be a city by Leon De la Rósa, illustrated by Gui.ra.ga7 (Second Edition)

Blue Rooms, Black Holes, White Lights by Belinda Subraman (Second Edition)

Scorpions by Joel Chace

Ghazals 1-59 and Other Poems by Sheila E. Murphy and Michelle Greenblatt

brain : storm by Michelle Greenblatt (Second Edition, originally anabasis Press)